California Quails

Julie Murray

Abdo Kids Junior
is an Imprint of Abdo Kids
abdobooks.com

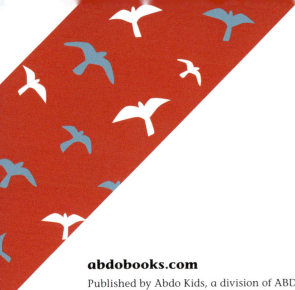

abdobooks.com

Published by Abdo Kids, a division of ABDO, P.O. Box 398166, Minneapolis, Minnesota 55439. Copyright © 2022 by Abdo Consulting Group, Inc. International copyrights reserved in all countries. No part of this book may be reproduced in any form without written permission from the publisher. Abdo Kids Junior™ is a trademark and logo of Abdo Kids.

Printed in the United States of America, North Mankato, Minnesota.

052021

092021

Photo Credits: Alamy, Getty Images, iStock, Shutterstock

Production Contributors: Teddy Borth, Jennie Forsberg, Grace Hansen

Design Contributors: Candice Keimig, Pakou Moua

Library of Congress Control Number: 2020947500
Publisher's Cataloging-in-Publication Data

Names: Murray, Julie, author.
Title: California quails / by Julie Murray
Description: Minneapolis, Minnesota : Abdo Kids, 2022 | Series: State birds | Includes online resources and index.
Identifiers: ISBN 9781098207144 (lib. bdg.) | ISBN 9781098207984 (ebook) | ISBN 9781098208400 (Read-to-Me ebook)
Subjects: LCSH: State birds--Juvenile literature. | Quails--Juvenile literature. | Birds--Behavior--United States--Juvenile literature.
Classification: DDC 598.297--dc23

Table of Contents

California Quails.....4

State Bird..........22

Glossary............23

Index 24

Abdo Kids Code.....24

California Quails

California quails live in the western US.

5

They live in low **brush** areas.

Some live in busy cities.

7

They are round-shaped birds.

Females are brownish gray in color. Males have more head **markings**.

The birds have a topknot.

They are fast runners.

They do not usually fly.

They scratch and peck for food.

They eat seeds and leaves.

17

They build nests. The nest is on the ground. It is lined with grass.

The eggs are cream in color.

They have brown spots.

Chicks hatch in 20 days.

State Bird

CA
California

22

Glossary

brush
a thick group of small trees, bushes, or other plants growing together.

chick
a bird that has just hatched or a young bird.

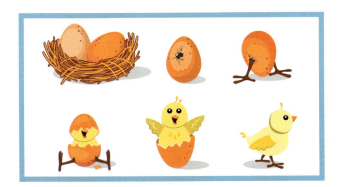

hatch
to come out of an egg.

marking
a pattern of marks or coloring on an animal.

Index

chicks 20

color 10, 20

eggs 20

females 10

food 16

habitat 6

males 10

markings 10, 20

movement 14

nest 18

shape 8

United States 4

Visit **abdokids.com** to access crafts, games, videos, and more!

Use Abdo Kids code **SCK7144** or scan this QR code!